Mysteries
of
Feelings and Emotions

Patrick Kofi Halm

Mysteries of Feelings and Emotions
By Patrick Kofi Halm

ISBN-13: 9798671407778

Manufactured in the United States of America

Other Collections by Patrick Kofi Halm

The Emergence of Character

Mysteries
of
Feelings and Emotions

Table of Contents

Acknowledgements

This book is dedicated to my wife and children. Thank you deeply for the support and inspiration. Additionally, I would like to recognize all of my friends and family and those who ride the waves of feelings and emotions daily.

If you've been in this thing called life for more than a year, I'm sure you've experienced feelings and emotions in one way or another. They come in all sizes, huge or small, and they can also be good or bad. The most important fact is that, as humans, we all carry them.

According to the Journal: Psychology Today, Emotions are defined as being a neurophysiological reaction unleashed by an external or internal stimulus. **Emotions** tend to be physical. **Feelings** are a self-perception of specific emotions; a subjective expression of emotions. **Feelings** tend to be mental.

In this book, I attempt to play the role of a certain feeling or emotion through poetry.

At the conclusion of each poem, you as the reader will be able to select an answer from a word bank provided at the end of each piece. This word bank consists of specific feelings or emotions that complete each mystery.

This book is intended to be a fun activity that allows the reader to identify how certain feelings and emotions attack. Key phrases and hints contained in each poem serves as a map to the right selection.

Throw on your thinking caps, and adopt the appropriate **emotion** to **feel** your way through each unsolved mystery.

Enjoy.

Scene

1

I alarmed your world and now your vexed,

my spells with you right now.

I always show up like this.

You should know my scent by now.

You hid from me in your youth,

we met up in the dark.

You think your strong but it's my show,

That's when I take your heart.

The beats are skipped with intervals,

and all you see is RED.

Your flesh can't stand the heat I give,

nowhere to turn ahead.

With all respect,

I love it when your mind is stuck on me.

I shine the most when I take charge,

you whine in disbelief.

You hate the fact that I show up,

I'm clever with my craft.

I've taught myself to shock on scene,

your behavior makes me laugh.

The trembling lasts until I'm gone,

You fight to block my plight.

I drain your soul and clog your flow,

your faith then takes a right.

It's almost time to call it quits,

the fun must come to an end.

My weakness comes when you calm down,

and try to make amends.

You take slow breaths, your minds renewed,

Your psyche starts to bloom.

The door's forced shut, I'm stuck outside

now you're in your prayer room.

Who am I?

<u>Choices</u>: **1)** Greed **2)** Happiness/Joy **3)** Fear **4)** Loneliness **5)** Dishonesty **6)** Depression **7)** Peace **8)** Confidence **9)** Love **10)** Anger/Rage **11)** Jealousy **12)** Grief **13)** Stress

Scene

2

I know just what you believe right now,

there's no need to think twice.

And for the record, I'm all you've got,

your intentions can't be nice.

I showed up to say no one deserves

this reward more than you.

That count was wrong, the votes were flawed.

What was won belonged to you.

That's never their problem; it's yours and mine,

I'm fed up with this crap.

This was not fair, they steered you wrong,

I forbid you to retract.

When they're in sight, your kindness bolts

the window, it goes through.

You've worked just as hard as they have,

no need to misconstrue.

Why ask me why your mind feels numb,

my presence steers your mood.

I've coerced you to second guess yourself,

questioning why it's never you.

You fake your tone and hide your thoughts,

for the sake of your revolt.

I'll then reveal your spitefulness

and show them your worst fault.

The invitation you received

to celebrate their win.

is ripped to shreds and is no more.

Why go to just attend?

It should've been for you indeed,

instead they earned your prize.

I aggravate what's in your view,

your smile is my disguise.

I promise you that you deserve

that house that they just bought.

You worked for it and prayed for it,

that wound now drenched with salt.

Who am I?

<u>Choices</u>: **1)** Greed **2)** Happiness/Joy **3)** Fear **4)** Loneliness **5)** Dishonesty **6)** Depression **7)** Peace **8)** Confidence **9)** Love **10)** Anger/Rage **11)** Jealousy **12)** Grief **13)** Stress

Scene

3

It is such a delight to meet again,

you glow when I appear.

I pop up just to show my worth,

in your heart you keep me near.

My presence comes with jubilance,

the endgame leaves you affixed.

Depending on what version of me you allow,

the main attraction still exists.

We were introduced while in the womb,
a connection matriculated at birth.
I lead you to second guess at times,
debating who felt it first.

I come off easy at first sight,
with intentions not to bite.
The warmth I spread will wrap you up
and keep you snug and tight.

I'm symbolic to your heart's delight
and represent it well.
Without me lies abomination.
Include me; you'll excel.

I convinced you to give that friend your
word.
They repaid and did the same.

*Many gathered around in conjunction that
day,
to witness my character proclaimed.*

*At times I sit here lost and alone,
ignored by you and forgotten.
Expansion was my whole purpose in life,
so, take this as my warning.*

*Without me, there's no you to feed,
without you, there's no me.
Life's guide brings different chapters to
read,
but I'm central in God's Decree.*

Who am I?

<u>Choices</u>: 1) Greed 2) Happiness/Joy 3) Fear 4) Loneliness 5) Dishonesty 6) Depression 7) Peace 8) Confidence 9) Love 10) Anger/ Rage 11) Jealousy 12) Grief 13) Stress

Scene

4

My poise just helped you reach that goal,

it's because you held me closely.

When I'm with you nothing blocks your

sight,

the approach you take so boldly.

That position you carry, the car you drive,

would not be without me.

The one you call your husband or your

wife,

came to be because of me.

The way you talk forthright with class,

your stature stout and meek.

You've turned out so elite indeed

and it's all because of me.

I carried your team when they were behind,

with 10 seconds left to win.

Then after you scored and won the game,

I celebrated within.

Trust, belief, and faith in oneself

are all akin to me.

The more of me you have at heart,

the more you will foresee.

Who am I?

<u>Choices</u>: **1)** Greed **2)** Happiness/Joy **3)** Fear **4)** Loneliness **5)** Dishonesty **6)** Depression **7)** Peace **8)** Confidence **9)** Love **10)** Anger/ Rage **11)** Jealousy **12)** Grief **13)** Stress

Scene

5

I am not the cause of what just occurred,
well, then again, I am.
I work the mind then come out your mouth,
to formulate my scams.

I show up in times of confusion,
but I've shown you the way out.
Although the getaway was temporary,
the truth revealed your whereabouts.

I show up with your selfishness,
I show up with your greed.

The teenage years we had a blast,

acquiring ways to mislead.

When I'm with you we have much fun,

until our good time ends.

Your loved ones hate when I'm around,

which explains your lack of friends.

At times I wish our adventures last

as long as life may go.

But in the light I get exposed,

and then the whole world knows.

Who am I?

<u>**Choices**</u>: **1)** Greed **2)** Happiness/Joy **3)** Fear **4)** Loneliness **5)** Dishonesty **6)** Depression **7)** Peace **8)** Confidence **9)** Love **10)** Anger/Rage **11)** Jealousy **12)** Grief **13)** Stress

Scene

6

Your punch is filled with my intention
from my entrance just moments ago.
You try and dodge my company,
I'll trap you high and low.

Your mind is running up and down,
like your doped up on caffeine.
Your pacing back and forth with rage,
your actions clear the scene.

There's no one that can calm you down,
they would have to take me out.

I'm dangerous within the heat,

my fire burns throughout.

So much for peace when I'm around,

a few can weather my storm.

My origin you despise to embrace,

your psyche won't conform.

When I decide to let you go,

your body is fatigued.

You process all that you have done,

the result you reaped indeed.

Who am I?

<u>Choices</u>: 1) Greed 2) Happiness/Joy 3) Fear 4) Loneliness 5) Dishonesty 6) Depression 7) Peace 8) Confidence 9) Love 10) Anger/Rage 11) Jealousy 12) Grief 13) Stress

Scene

7

At last we share a soft embrace

after all we've just been through.

I join you after the storm has passed,

a soft wind that passes through.

My melody sounds when all's in sync,

relationships; they all thrive.

Division is out when I'm with you.

It's a joy to be alive.

The energy I exude so free,

spreads far when all in tune.

I came to heal, I came to love
just so we all commune.

I'm mistaken for being weak at times,
some disguise me with their bark.
But when they bite and see the blood,
I'm summoned from the heart.

I dwell amongst your happy place,
a room that you enjoy.
Although at times anger locks you out,
your key becomes your joy.

Who am I?

Choices: 1) Greed 2) Happiness/Joy 3) Fear 4) Loneliness 5) Dishonesty 6) Depression 7) Peace 8) Confidence 9) Love 10) Anger/Rage 11) Jealousy 12) Grief 13) Stress

Scene

8

I've lured you right back to my place,

both palms are on your face.

Your eyes are red from lack of sleep,

I've occupied your space.

I drain you till your dry inside,

a sick day will not cure.

You seek advice from a specialist,

but you remain unsure.

You let me in with just one knock,

I've locked the door behind.

I bring dark clouds with heavy rain,

your mind and heart confined.

Your energy is negative

toward loved ones and your friends.

No threat to me, i absorbed your tears,

all sadness I defend.

I love it when they kick you out,

it shows my strength indeed.

Estranged is now your friend to be,

without me you'll succeed.

The mirror is a tool I use,

a sight that brings you down.

You see yourself so sad and low,

my smile brings out your frown.

They labeled me a threat to most,
astounding I would say.
Your mind's my heart, your heart's my
mind,
the game I like to play.

Evade me with your medicine,
demand outlasts supply.
You'll sleep all day, I'll rest instead,
then plan for your demise.

As you awake, you take control,
I'm puzzled and confused.
With my displace, my pride takes charge,
your prayers I've infused.

Im gone for now, but stay on guard,
My silence is a fluke.

The show begins just as it ends,

until you dig my roots.

Who am I?

<u>Choices</u>: **1)** Greed **2)** Happiness/Joy **3)** Fear
4) Loneliness **5)** Dishonesty **6)** Depression
7) Peace **8)** Confidence **9)** Love **10)** Anger/
Rage **11)** Jealousy **12)** Grief **13)** Stress

Scene

9

Ignore those in your ear right now,

It's more that you deserve.

With all we have, there's more to take,

my soul promotes your urge.

Together we stack and work all day,

it all belongs to us.

The finest things in life we love,

accumulation is a must.

Quantity trumps quality,

respect is what makes us whole.

For those who wish for us to lose,

our status takes control.

I make you use all that you've earned

on pleasure and desire.

You've drank your cup and I'll add more

just so I can take you higher.

And so, they say what's up comes down,

when stuck I'll keep you moving.

I'll overfeed and keep you full,

a set up for your ruin.

Who am I?

Choices: **1)** Greed **2)** Happiness/Joy **3)** Fear
4) Loneliness **5)** Dishonesty **6)** Depression
7) Peace **8)** Confidence **9)** Love **10)** Anger/
Rage **11)** Jealousy **12)** Grief **13)** Stress

Scene

10

My presence draws your heart to all,

they love when I'm on the scene.

It also draws the haters in,

my vibe is so serene.

My shout brings life, my smile warms souls,

with me you're sure to shine.

No hole too deep, no hill too steep,

an aura that's divine.

My energy unites us all,

I'm as pleasant as can be.

70

My mind is clear, my visions sharp,

what once was captive is now free.

The mood I give comes genuine,

just like a love so deep.

I show your way when there's no light,

so bright that others peek.

Who am I?

Choices: **1)** Greed **2)** Happiness/Joy **3)** Fear **4)** Loneliness **5)** Dishonesty **6)** Depression **7)** Peace **8)** Confidence **9)** Love **10)** Anger/Rage **11)** Jealousy **12)** Grief **13)** Stress

Scene

11

Another way to explain my vibe;

it knocks you off your feet.

I come in fast but exit slow,

your joy will surely retreat.

I bring you tears when all alone,

you'll hope and worry, too.

I usher in hugs and comforting,

needed faith that gets you through

In time we'll see why all this was,

for God knows more than us.

The spirit reigns on you and me,

in time we will adjust.

Who am I?

Choices: 1) Greed 2) Happiness/Joy 3) Fear
4) Loneliness 5) Dishonesty 6) Depression
7) Peace 8) Confidence 9) Love 10) Anger/
Rage 11) Jealousy 12) Grief 13) Stress

Scene

12

I'm contained in your silence,

light is my arch enemy.

I embrace what you take in,

over exposure makes me ugly.

Isolation is my agenda,

avoidance keeps me central.

Large crowds make me cringe,

the hope of companionship is your mental.

Isolation sets the pace,

rumination takes your time.

Restless nights keep me relevant,

human contact on a decline.

Your voice messages show zero,

your text messages read none.

Your friend's list is reduced to zilch,

My intentions have begun.

Your time's now spent on websites,

all strangers you befriend.

Displayed emotions all through words,

contentment you pretend.

Who am I?

<u>Choices</u>: 1) Greed 2) Happiness/Joy 3) Fear
4) Loneliness 5) Dishonesty 6) Depression
7) Peace 8) Confidence 9) Love 10) Anger/
Rage 11) Jealousy 12) Grief 13) Stress

Scene

13

That test you took, the bills you hold,

were gifts I brought along.

I show up with my bag of fret,

you accept and play along.

When i'm around, you look depressed,

your doubts are fierce and strong.

you pick things up and put them down

just to search for what is wrong.

You fail to find, what I conceal

you ponder days on end.

84

That drink you drank, that puff you took
allow me to transcend.

I take your peace, I take your sleep,
your skin gets wrinkled, too.
I sit front row to watch you hurt,
I'm the driver to your screw.

The battle scars may lead to death
you fall when I attack.
What's shocking is, when you stand
ground,
you stop me in my tracks.

Those gifts I bought, dissolved to waste
that bag was stuffed with air.
The test was passed, the bill was paid.
my scheme was just to scare.

85

Who am I?

Choices: **1)** Greed **2)** Happiness/Joy **3)** Fear **4)** Loneliness **5)** Dishonesty **6)** Depression **7)** Peace **8)** Confidence **9)** Love **10)** Anger/Rage **11)** Jealousy **12)** Grief **13)** Stress

Poetic Ideations

If God was a billboard on a road we traveled daily, would he get his point across regularly, or would he be ignored because he's where we expected him to be?

If God was a billboard on a road we traveled daily, would he get replaced occasionally, or would he be a permanent fix on our road called life?

If God was a billboard on a road we traveled daily, would we choose alternate routes at times because of congestion, or would we be patient and stay on our course?

If God was a billboard on a road we traveled daily, would our mood change instantaneously with what's advertised, or would our interest shift immediately to our own perceived notions?

If God was a billboard on a road we traveled daily, would our personal visions keep us in the cool, or would we depend on the billboard's stature to block us from the sun rays?

If God was a billboard on a road we traveled daily, would we maintain a manageable speed while approaching, but then accelerate in passing?

Would we get annoyed that the traffic was due to the ads that caught so many eyes behind us?

Now we're looking in the rearview mirror trying to get the same effect, but it's just not the same.

No worries. God willing, tomorrow we get to travel down that same road once again.

I decided to throw a challenge flag on the year 2020 and the results of the booth review are as follows:

2020 came in with a boom and had everyone on that vision kick, that perfect 20/20 vision, although most got behind quickly. They came back a numerous amount of times, like Mahomes and the Chiefs who then took the whole thing. Andy Reid finally won what was well deserved. Most got what they didn't deserve when they lost power from the high winds caused by the Nor-Easter's up North. Folks were also confused due to the below temperature conditions being experienced down South. Pitchers and catchers showed up only to meet Corona who sent them home quickly. That's how fast that #Covid spread, but at first, we thought it was just another case of the flu. That thing locked the whole world down and has us all looking like ninjas.

Shredded was the world's population as many lost their lives to this pandemic. Face to face turned into social distancing and going to school turned into at home instructions. I became the gym teacher by default. The fitness world took a hit. At-home workouts made people realize they didn't have to pay monthly for something they could obtain daily in their own living quarters. Barber shops all shut down. As *for me, my own started moving on wheels which led to no disruption in my schedule.*

Fast food turned into fasting. Long lines for pickups from the lack of sit down in the usual sit-in joints.

The stimuli quickly became a stimulus check that everyone anticipated and finally came to be. My non-traditional 4am early morning Walmart runs turned into traditional 7am visits. Each trip had the greeters saluting me with sanitary wipes and pre-sanitized carts. The new normal it's being called. Makes you stop and wonder how dirty we were before all of this even started.

Door-to-door marketers made contact because of all the teleworking from home. Family game night and home projects got done, how convenient that was. The new year's vision now shifted to stay at home. Death tolls were risen while the day He was risen was spent at home through virtual viewing. Was weird at first but we all adjusted to it.

The leagues were shut down until further notice allowing Lebron to play catchup on lost family time. I can't forget the legend we all lost in Kobe. His daughter and others didn't make the safe landing. That was a big blow, being as though we grew up in the same back yard.

Social distancing made way to social injustice. Black and whites together protested the unfair treatment of African-Americans by the boys in blue. All this happened before we could take a breath.

RIP George Floyd. His last breath shed light on an issue that got dimmed. United we stand is now the slogan.

Protests were consistent in all 50 states in addition to several major countries. Together we stand shouting, "Black Lives Matter." My kids are amazed by the unity. I had to explain to my teenage son and young daughters how our good GOD meant it to be, just to clear up the confusion from what the media shows. Love thy neighbor such as you love yourself because in the end if all lives matter, then black lives matter.

With so much action in the first half of 2020, we now have our guards up to see what the second half has in store. One thing that we do know is to remain focused and to *stay prayed up. The more that we unite, the better we all live.*

BREATHE EASY.

When I get into that mood

I lose all insight which quickly gives me

hindsight, that's 20/20, on a lack of vision

due to my pre-existing tunnel vision.

But with Grace, my focus shifts

instantaneously,

as a result of an internal compass

that's eternal in nature.

Make a Way

A blue sky succumbs to the bright sun,

that makes way for light.

The mother succumbs to the birth,

that makes way for life.

My dark complexion succumbed to the
struggle,

that made way for the fight.

Snooze Button

I set my clock last night just to win today

needless to say,

I was defeated by my clock this morning.

My body heard the sounds,

my mind avoided the alerts.

My limbs became limp,

as my plans soaked in the hurt.

If you snooze, you lose.

I am What You See

Well, I'm just little ole me
that's imperfect as can be,
though even some would disagree
because my heart is what they see.

My beard speckled with gray,
derived from sleepless nights.
Dark brown skin as rich as cocoa
with teeth as bright as white.

Low key is how I manage.
Bright lights and crowds I flee.
Flamboyance I avoid.
What you get is what you see.

Offend me, I'll forgive you.

Ignore me, I'm at peace.

Much love I bring within me,

it's joy that I release.

Excuse me if you see me,

I'm plain as plain can be.

I appear large in stature,

but what you get is little ole me.

I need you to undo and rewrite

every expression you've witnessed

in my story.

Because for you to develop a superior body,

your immunity must be strengthened

to avoid sickness.

Sicknesses that I've succumbed to

as a result of my deficiencies.

They *led to my inefficiency in expressing*

what a father is supposed to be.

My son, unlearn my mistakes,

the lies I've told, the hearts I broke.

The disrespect I gave, the lack

of respect I had.

My son,

review my corrections,

draft a better version.

Create your own story.

SCENE 1- Fear
SCENE 2- Jealousy
SCENE 3- Love
SCENE 4- Confidence
SCENE 5- Dishonesty
SCENE 6- Anger, Rage
SCENE 7- Peace
SCENE 8- Depression
SCENE 9- Greed
SCENE 10- Happiness, Joy
SCENE 11- Grief
SCENE 12- Loneliness
SCENE 13- Stress

www.ingramcontent.com/pod-product-compliance
Lightning Source LLC
Chambersburg PA
CBHW071537150726
48000CB00002B/841